Animal Lives

BEARS

Sally Morgan

QED Publishing

QED

Written by Sally Morgan
Designed by Tall Tree Books
Editor Christine Harvey
Map by PCGraphics (UK) Ltd

Creative Director Louise Morley
Editorial Manager Jean Coppendale

Printed and bound in China

Picture credits

Key: t = top, b = bottom, m = middle,
c = centre, l = left, r = right

Corbis /Joe McDonald 5, /Keren Su 6, /David
A. Northcott 7tr, /Raymond Gehman 24,
/Kevin Schafer 29
Ecoscene /Papilio Clive Druett 4, 30tl, /Papilio
Robert Pickett 9br, /Fritz Polking 10,/Papilio
Jamie Harron 15, 30b, /Michael Gore 16m,
/Wayne Lawler 18, /Fritz Polking 19, /Papilio
Robert Plckett 21, /Papilio Jamie Harron
26–27, /Visual & Written 28
Getty Images front cover Tom Walker /Wayne
R Bilenduke 1, 13tr, /Tom Walker 7br, /David E
Myers 8-9, /Stuart & Michele Westmorland
11m, /Art Wolfe 11, /Kathy Bushue 12–13,
30ml, /Wayne R Bilenduke 13tr, /Johnny
Johnson 14, /David E Myers 16–17, /Tom
Walker 20, /Johnny Johnson 22–23, /Art
Wolfe23t, /Art Wolfe23br
Still Pictures /Charlie Russell 25, /Fred
Bruemmer26br

The words in **bold** are
explained in the Glossary
on page 31.

Contents

The bear

Bears are some of the best-known animals in the world. Bears have a heavy body and thick legs. Their head is large and they have a big nose and small eyes. They have large feet called paws. Each of their toes ends in a long, sharp claw.

The brown bear has very thick, dark brown fur. It has a wide neck and powerful shoulders.

The sun bear gets its name from the markings on the front of its body.

Mammals

Bears belong to a group of animals called mammals. Like most mammals, female bears give birth to live young and produce milk for them. Bears are covered with fur. This helps them to stay warm. Their body temperature hardly changes, no matter what the temperature around them might be.

Bear types

There are eight species, or types, of bear. The most well-known are the polar bear, brown bear and giant panda. In North America, the brown bear is often called the grizzly bear.

Other species of bear are the American black bear, the Asian black bear, the sun bear, the sloth bear and the spectacled bear.

Most bears have fur that is black, brown or white. The polar bear is the only completely white bear.

Giant panda cubs stay with their mothers for up to three years.

Small bears

The Asian black bear, sun bear, sloth bear and spectacled bear are much smaller than the other bears. The sun bear is the smallest.

The sloth bear has no front teeth so it can suck up termites from their nests.

The American and Asian black bears look similar. However, the Asian black bear has a crescent-shaped white patch on its chest that gives it its other name – 'moon bear'.

American black bears can go without food for up to seven months during hibernation.

Bear

American black bears are not always black. They come in all shades of brown and a few are white!

fact

Where do you find bears?

Polar bears are found mainly in the Arctic, where it is cold all year round. Brown bears are found across North America, northern Europe and Asia. They live in different **habitats**, including forests and open ground. Giant pandas are found only in central China, where they live in bamboo forests.

Bear

Polar bears spend as much time on the ice as they do on land. Small, soft bumps on the pads of their feet stop them from slipping.

fact

Polar bears are found in Alaska, Canada, Russia, Denmark and Norway.

North America

Europe

Asia

Atlantic Ocean

Africa

Pacific Ocean

Pacific Ocean

South America

Indian Ocean

Australia

Southern Ocean

Antarctica

Areas where bears are found.

Other bears

Spectacled bears live in forests in South America. Sloth bears are found in different habitats in India. Sun bears live in forests in South East Asia. Black bears live in forest areas in America and Asia.

The American black bear is found across North America and in Mexico.

9

Living in the Arctic

Polar bears are well suited to living in the icy world of the Arctic. Polar bears have large bodies that are covered in thick, white fur. The only parts of their bodies not covered in fur are their black noses and the pads on the bottom of their feet.

The polar bear's white fur is good camouflage against the snow.

Keeping warm

Polar bears have black skin. Black is a good colour in the Arctic, because it **absorbs** heat. Beneath their skin is a thick layer of fat called blubber. The fat helps to keep the bear warm, as it stops heat escaping from their bodies.

Bear

Polar bears are champion swimmers. They have been known to swim more than 96km without a rest. They can swim at speeds of up to 10km per hour.

fact

A polar bear is so well **insulated** with fur and fat that it loses hardly any heat. In fact, it is not unusual for an adult bear to overheat when it runs.

A polar bear's feet are partly webbed.

Polar bears lie on the ice to cool down.

Beginning life

A female bear is ready to mate when she reaches four to five years of age. After mating, she is **pregnant** for seven to eight months.

A newborn bear cub is small. It is about the size of a guinea pig. Cubs are born blind and without fur. They **suckle** their mother's milk for six months before they start to eat solid food.

Bear

Most bear cubs weigh between 200 and 300g. Polar bear cubs are slightly heavier at 600 and 700g.

fact

A female bear gives birth to a litter of one to three cubs.

Bear cubs stay close to their mother for the first few months.

Dens

Bears that live in cold climates spend the winter in a **den**. Their cubs are born in the den in the middle of winter. The cubs stay with their mother in the den for three months. In early spring, the temperature gets warmer and the bear leads her cubs outside for the first time.

In the Arctic, the female polar bear digs out a hole under the snow where she gives birth to her cubs.

Growing up

When the cubs come out of the den their mother shows them what foods are good to eat. After six months, bear cubs grow their adult teeth.

The cubs spend a lot of time playing with each other. The mother growls or grunts at her cubs if they misbehave. If they do not listen to her warnings she knocks them over with her paw.

Bear cubs follow their mother everywhere, learning from everything she does.

Living in territories

Bear cubs stay with their mother for up to four years. Then the young bears move away.

Adult bears live on their own in one area. This is their **territory**. The female bear raises her cubs on her own, without any help from the male bear. When the young bears leave their mother, they have to find a territory of their own.

Bear

Most bears live between 20 to 30 years in the wild. Brown bears have lived to 47 years of age in zoos.

fact

Polar bear cubs like to play-fight. They often stand up like boxers or roll on the ground like wrestlers.

15

Hunting

Polar bears and brown bears are **predators**. They have sharp teeth and long claws to grip their **prey**. The polar bear is a **carnivore**. It hunts by stalking or by lying in wait for its prey. Sometimes, the polar bear will creep over the ice towards its prey, charging when it is close. At other times, it sits beside a hole in the ice, waiting for a seal to come up to breathe. When the seal comes up, the bear bites it and drags it onto the ice. Polar bear cubs learn to hunt by watching their mother.

A seal provides enough food to feed a polar bear for about eight days.

Fishing for food

Brown bears feed on a variety of foods, such as fish, insects and berries. They are **omnivores**. In autumn, they fish in rivers. The bears wade into the water and catch the salmon as they swim past. The young cubs practise by standing in shallow water, trying to catch the salmon.

Bear
facts

- A brown bear may eat up to 16kg of food each day.

- Polar bears can catch small whales under the ice.

Brown bears grip the slippery salmon in their claws or teeth.

17

Eating

Brown bears and polar bears have four long teeth called canines at the front of their mouth. They use these teeth to grab their prey. They also have large teeth called molars that crush bones and slice through meat.

Smaller bears eat a mixed diet of insects, fruits and honey. The sloth bear breaks open termite nests with its sharp claws and sucks up hundreds of termites. The sun bear spends much of the day in the trees searching for food. It sticks its tongue into holes to find termites and to lick up honey from bees' nests.

The sun bear uses its long tongue to find food.

The giant panda

Giant pandas are the odd bears out, as they are **herbivores**. They eat only plants, especially bamboo shoots. They are born with a special bone in their wrists that sticks out. They use this bone, together with their thumbs, to grip bamboo stems. Giant pandas have strong jaws and cheek muscles to crush the thick stalks.

Giant pandas spend at least 16 hours each day eating bamboo.

Bear senses

Like human babies, bear cubs are born with all their senses and have to learn to use them. Polar bears have the best eyesight and can see well underwater. Most bears are short-sighted. This means they can see things that are close to them very well, for example food, but they are not very good at seeing things that are in the distance.

A bear's sense of smell is better than its sight.

Smell

A bear's sense of smell is better than a human's. Bears rely on their sense of smell to find food, identify their cubs and to find a mate. A good sense of smell allows them to detect and avoid danger, in the form of other bears and humans. A polar bear has a very good sense of smell and can detect its prey on the ice many kilometres away.

Bears leave their scent around the edge of their territory to let other bears know they should not come onto it.

Bear

Bears have been known to detect a human scent more than 14 hours after the person has passed along a trail.

fact

21

Moving

Bears walk slowly with their heads swinging gently from side to side. Most bears walk a bit like humans. They walk on the soles of their feet with their heels touching the ground first. Bears can also stand on their back feet and walk upright for short distances.

Although they walk slowly, some bears can run fast. An American black bear can run at 56km per hour for a short distance. That is about as fast as a horse or a deer.

Bears can run faster than humans. Once they start running they find it difficult to stop quickly.

Polar bears can swim for long distances and even dive under the ice.

Swimming and climbing

Polar bears are excellent swimmers. They swim by paddling with their huge front paws. They use their back legs to steer.

Many bears can climb, too. The sun bear has very long claws to grip the trunks of trees as it climbs. Sometimes it hugs the tree with its front legs and hauls itself up with its teeth!

American black bears climb into trees to find food such as buds, fruits and nuts.

23

Hibernation

Black and brown bears that live in colder parts of the world spend the winter in a deep sleep. This sleep is called hibernation. Bears hibernate because the weather is too cold for them and there is no food. Polar bears do not hibernate. They are active all year round.

A female American black bear and her cub have crawled under a large log to hibernate.

Getting ready to hibernate

In autumn, adult bears and cubs eat a lot of food to build up their body fat, ready for their hibernation. Then they look for a place to hibernate, such as a cave or a hollow under a fallen tree. Bears spend up to six months hibernating, without food or water. They live off their body fat. Female bears give birth to their cubs while hibernating. The cubs then hibernate with their mother the following winter.

Bear

It is not unusual for a bear to lose one third of its body weight while it is hibernating.

fact

Spirit bears are white-coloured black bears. Spirit bears are very rare.

Bears and people

Bears can be dangerous animals. The female bear is especially dangerous when she has cubs. She defends her cubs from predators, such as wolves and mountain lions. She will also attack humans if they come too close to her cubs.

Some bears have learned that where there are people, there will be food. They raid campsites and cars looking for food. Some visit rubbish dumps to find food.

Polar bears visit rubbish dumps to find food.

Bears in towns

Some bears go into towns and villages looking for food. People living in these areas try to stop the bears. They make sure the bears cannot find food or rubbish. They use special bins that the bears cannot get into.

Many bears are attracted to places in the countryside where people have dumped rubbish.

Bear

Because bears cannot see things in the distance very well, they may mistake a person for a predator or another bear, and attack them by mistake.

fact

Bears under threat

The number of bears around the world has fallen in the last 100 years. There were once 100 000 brown bears in North America; now there are only a few thousand. The rarest bear is the giant panda – there are only 1000 left.

Bears have been hunted by humans for sport, but in some areas, such as northern Canada, tourists travel to watch bears in their natural habitat. Special trucks called polar rovers take them out on the ice to see the polar bears.

People are not allowed to get too close or to get out of the polar rover because polar bears are very dangerous.

Habitats

Bears have lost their **habitats** because forests have been cleared for timber. Giant panda bears are under threat because there are very few bamboo forests left.

Polar bears are suffering because of climate change. This means that the ice breaks up much earlier each year, which stops the polar bears from hunting.

Today, many bears are protected. They live in national parks and nature reserves where they cannot be hunted.

The spectacled bear has white markings around its nose and eyes. It lives in forests in South America.

Bear fact

An adult polar bear's only real enemies are human hunters. It is very rare for polar bears to be attacked by other bears.

29

Life cycle

A female bear is pregnant for 8 months. She gives birth to between 1 and 3 cubs. The cubs drink their mother's milk for as long as 4 years. Then they leave and find a place to live on their own. Bears live between 20 and 30 years of age in the wild.

Six-month-old cubs

Young bears love to play-fight

An adult bear